Tricks and Flips

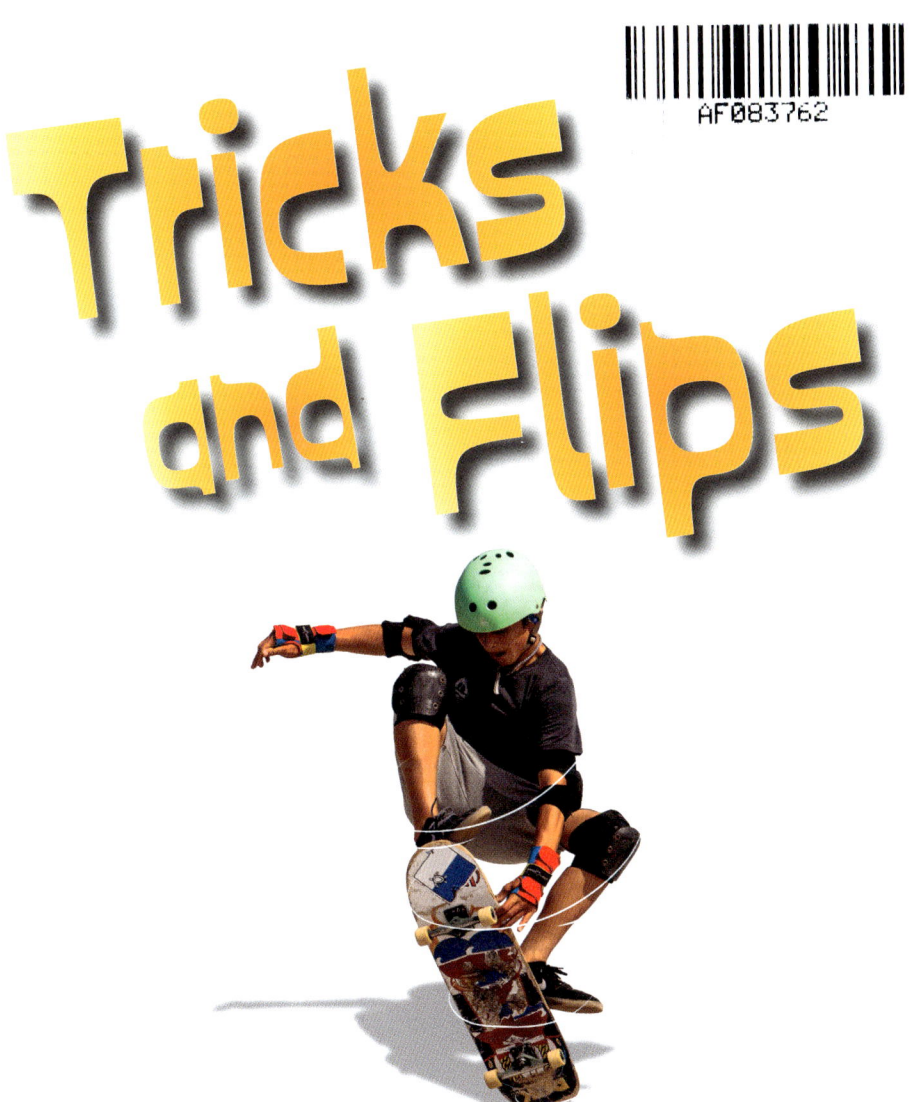

Written by Abbie Rushton
Illustrated by Ángeles Peinador

Collins

flip up high

spin on the spot

flip up high

spin on the spot

a trick on the bench

a jump from the steps

a trick on the bench

a jump from the steps

a high flip

a back bend

a high flip

a back bend

skid on the rim

jump and grab the boot

skid on the rim

jump and grab the boot

a quick spin

a trick on one hand

a quick spin

a trick on one hand

Review: After reading

Use your assessment from hearing the children read to choose any GPCs, words or tricky words that need additional practice.

Read 1: Decoding
- Turn to pages 2 and 3. Point to **flip** and model sounding out (*f/l/i/p*) then blending to read the whole word. (*flip*)
- Ask the children to read these words, sounding out then blending:

  jump   **bend**   **grab**   **hand**
- Say: Can you blend in your head silently when you read these words aloud?
- Ask the children to read pages 6 and 7, checking that they don't miss sounding out any of the consonants.

Read 2: Vocabulary
- Look back through the book and discuss the pictures. Encourage the children to talk about details that stand out for them. Use a dialogic talk model to expand on their ideas and recast them in full sentences as naturally as possible.
- Work together to expand vocabulary by naming objects in the pictures that children do not know.
- On page 14, discuss the meaning of **rim**. Say: A rim is the edge of something. Ask: Where is the rim here? (e.g. *the edge of the skate park ramp*)

Read 3: Comprehension
- Ask the children to talk about any activities in the book that they have seen in real life. Prompt with questions, such as: Where was it? What parts of their body did they use? Did they use special equipment? Discuss how the stunts in this book can be dangerous and are performed by experts. Children should not attempt these stunts themselves.
- Discuss what is the same about all the activities in the book. (e.g. *they need lots of practice, they need special movements*) Remind them of the book title and ask whether they think the activities are **tricks** and why.
- Use the pictures on pages 22 and 23 to model how to recap the content of the book. Ask the children to have a go.